Now I Know

About:
- Letters
- Numbers
- Shapes
- Colors
- Sports
- Instruments
- Animals
- And much more

Written by: Heddrick McBride
Illustrations: New Way Solutions
Cover: Alex Baranov

Letters

Aa

airplane

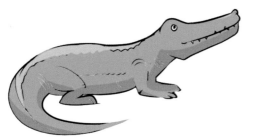

alligator

apple

Letters

Bb

ballerina

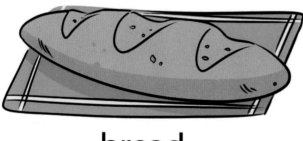

bread

banana

Letters

Cc

carrots

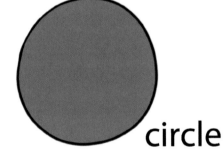

circle

car

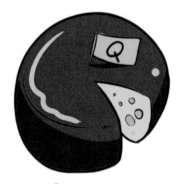

cheese

Dd

door

doctor

drummer

ducks

Letters

Ee

elephant

egg

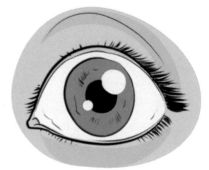

eye

Letters

F f

fish

football

fork

Letters

Gg

grapes

giraffe

grass

Letters

Hh

horse

hat

house

Letters

I i

ice cream

igloo

Letters

J j

jelly beans

jacket

juice

Letters

Kk

kangaroo

kite

knife

Letters

L l

leaf

lemon

lion

lollipop

Letters

Mm

milk

monkey

mountain

Letters

Nn

nest

nose

Letters

Oo

octagon

onion

oranges

owl

Letters

Pp

pig

pear

pumpkin

pizza

Letters

Qq

Queen

Letters

Rr

rabbit

rainbow

rectangle

ring

Letters

S s

star

square

strawberry

sun

Letters

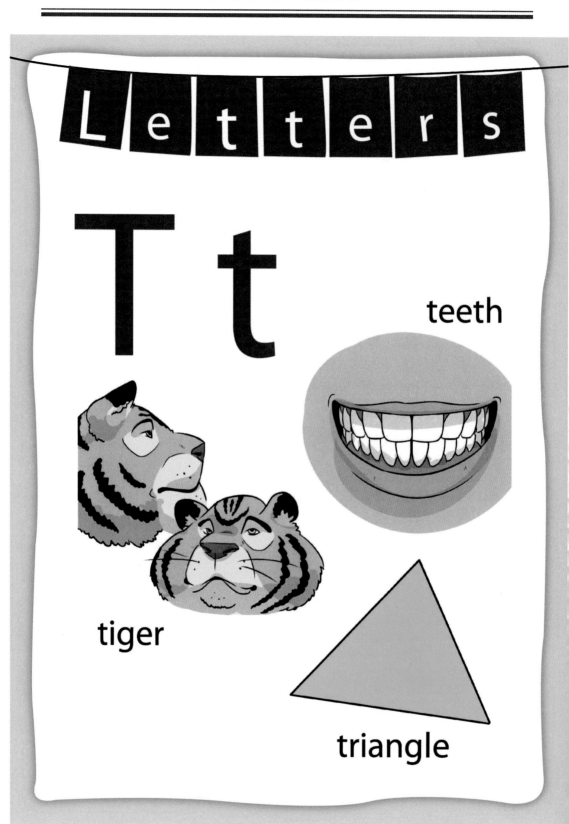

T t

teeth

tiger

triangle

Letters

U u

umbrella

unicorn

Letters

Vv

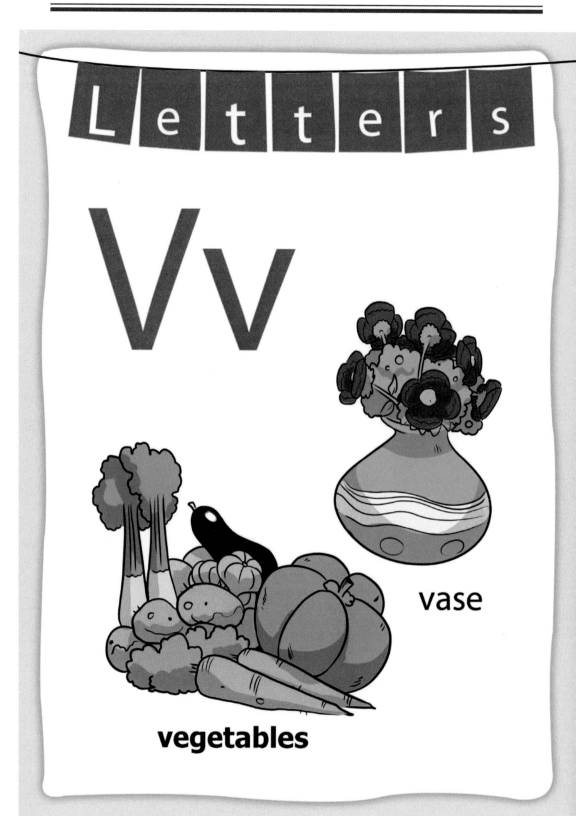

vase

vegetables

Letters

Ww

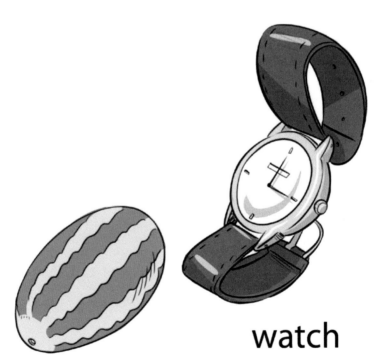

watch

watermelon

Letters

Xx

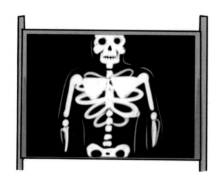

x-ray

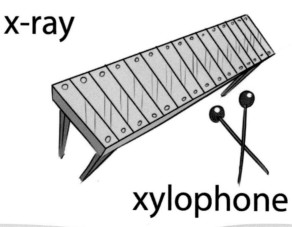

xylophone

Letters

Yy

Yellow

yo-yo

Letters

Zz

zoo

zebra

Numbers

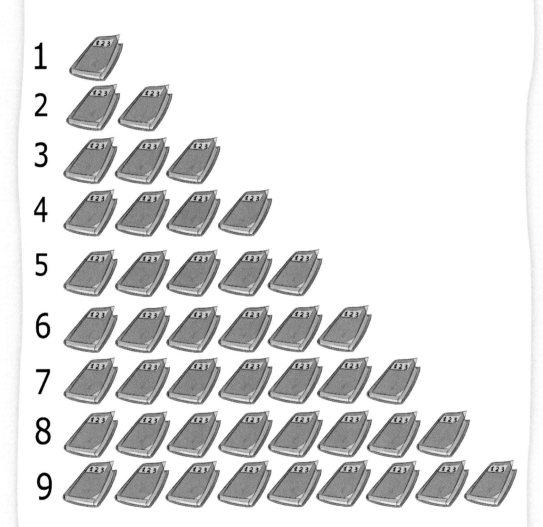

1
2
3
4
5
6
7
8
9

SHAPES

Circle	Rectangle	Octagon

Squares	Stars	Triangle

Letters

Colors

| Red | Orange | Yellow | Green |

| Blue | Black | Brown | Pink |

| Purple | Gold | Silver | Gray |

FRUITS

Apple	Banana	Cherries

Grapes	Lemon	Oranges

Pineapple	Watermelon

VEGETABLES

Broccoli	Carrots	Corn

Peas	String Beans

SPORTS

Baseball	Basketball	Soccer

Ice Skating	Golf	Tennis

INSTRUMENTS

Clarinet	Drums	Flute

Guitar	Harp	Piano

Saxophone	Xylophone

ANIMALS

Alligator	Cat	Cow

Dog	Duck	Elephant

ANIMALS

Frog	Giraffe	Horse

Kangaroo	Lion	Zebra

EVERYDAY FOODS

Bread	Cheeseburger	Cereal

Cheese	Chicken	Cookies

Eggs	French Fries

EVERYDAY DRINKS

Coffee	Soda

Hot Chocolate	Milk

Tea	Water

THINGS THAT WE USE TO EAT AND DRINK

Bowl	Fork	Glass

Napkin	Knife	Plate

Spoon

THINGS THAT WE USE TO STAY CLEAN AND NEAT

Comb	Brush	Toothbrush

Shower	Soap

Towel	Toothpaste

DAYS OF THE WEEK

Sunday
Monday
Tuesday
Wednesday
Thursday
Friday
Saturday

BODY PARTS

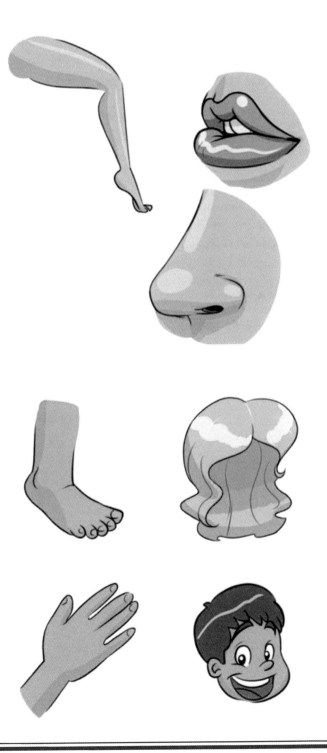

Made in the USA
Lexington, KY
24 November 2019